# Dangerous Curves

## Hot Sexy Plus-Size Lingerie Girls Models Pictures

By **PHOTO ART LOVER**

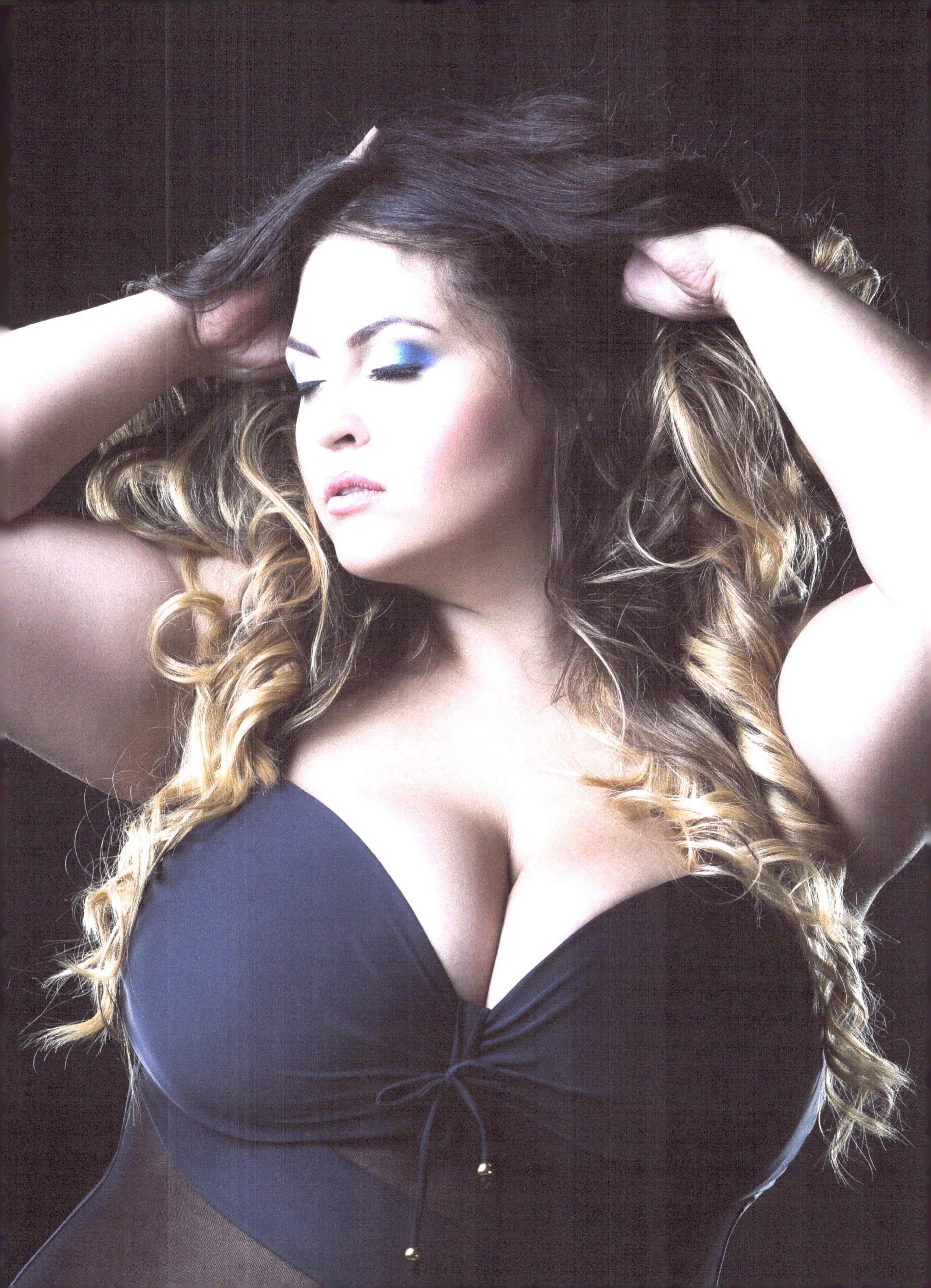

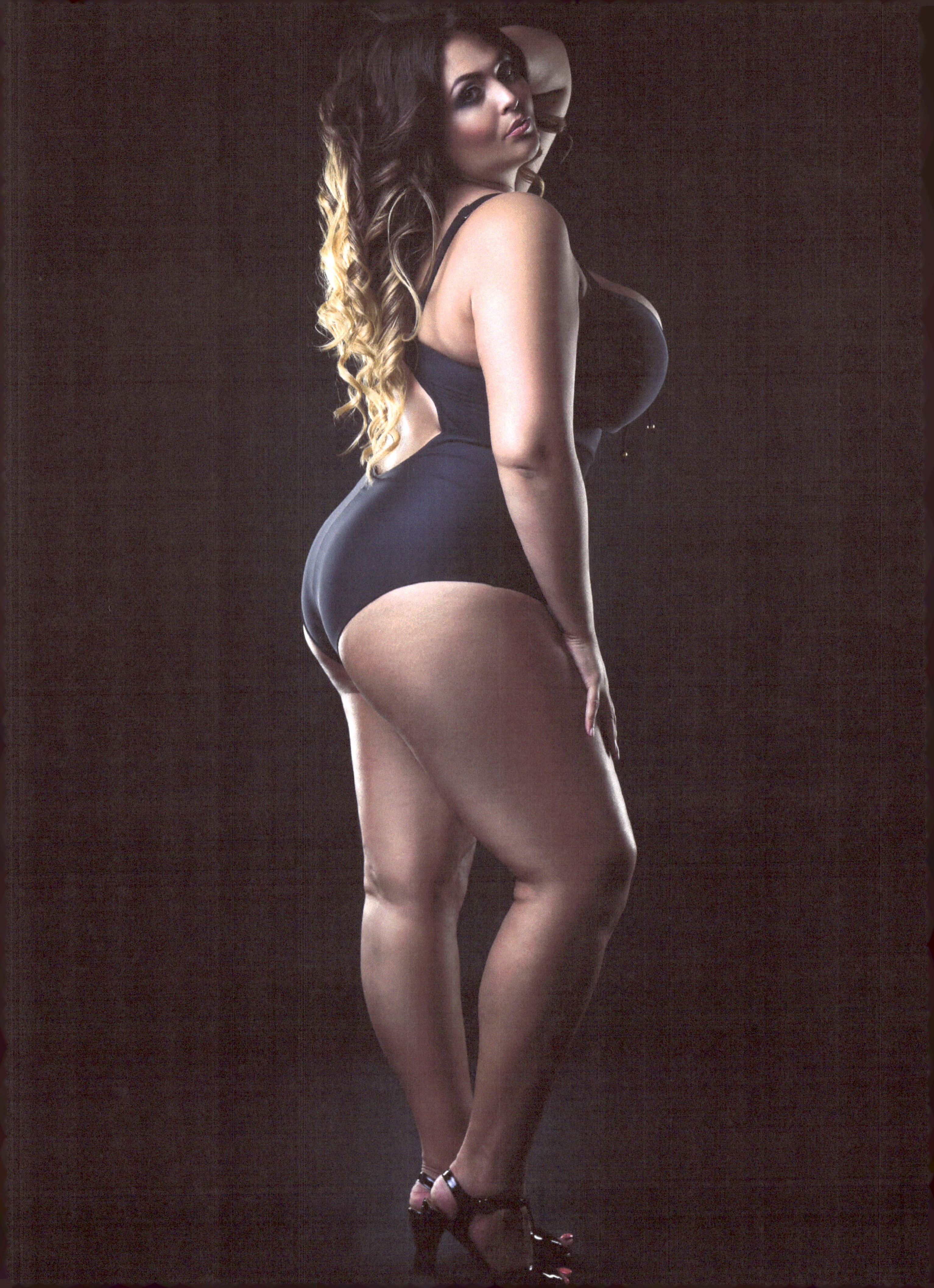

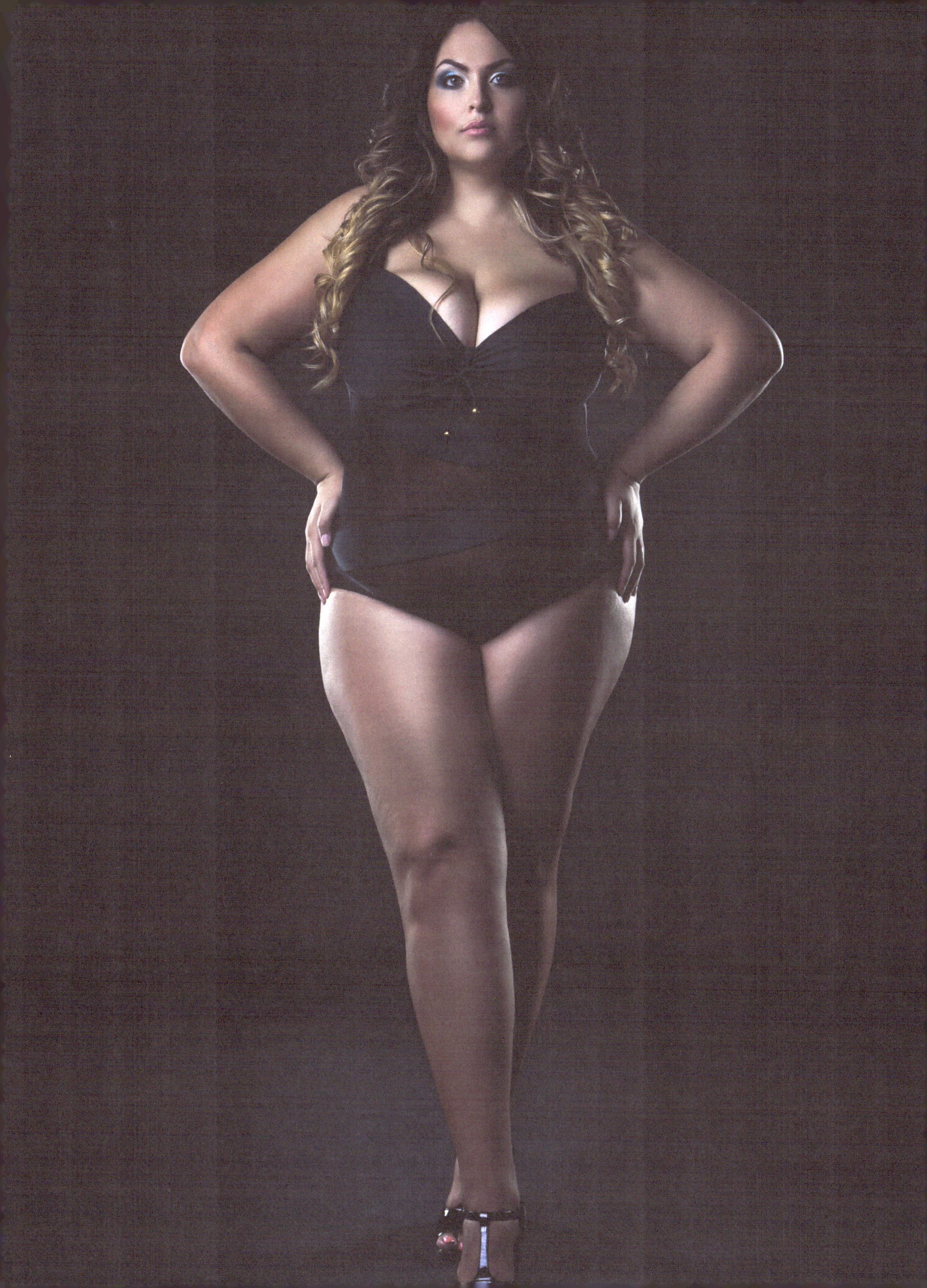

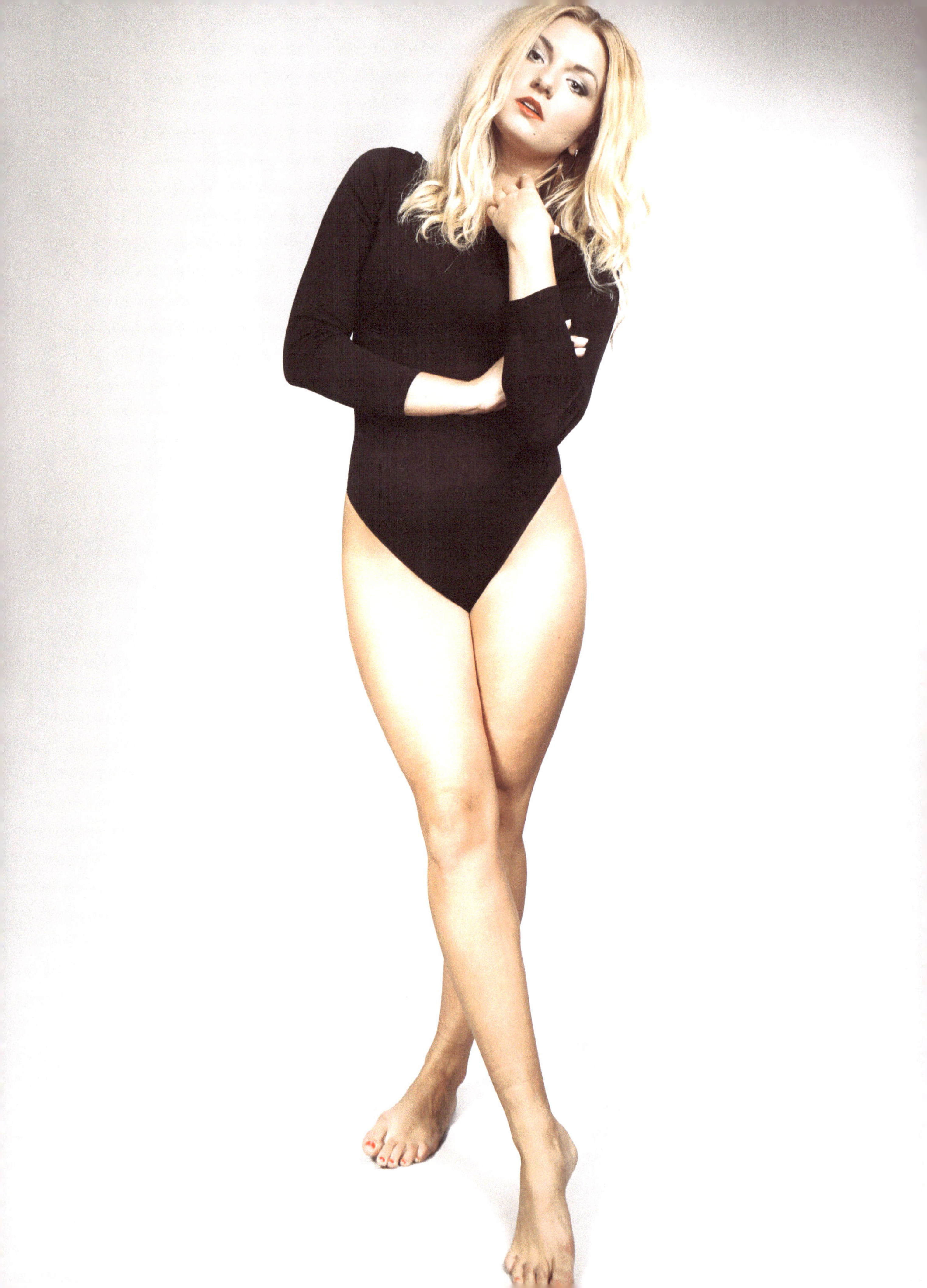

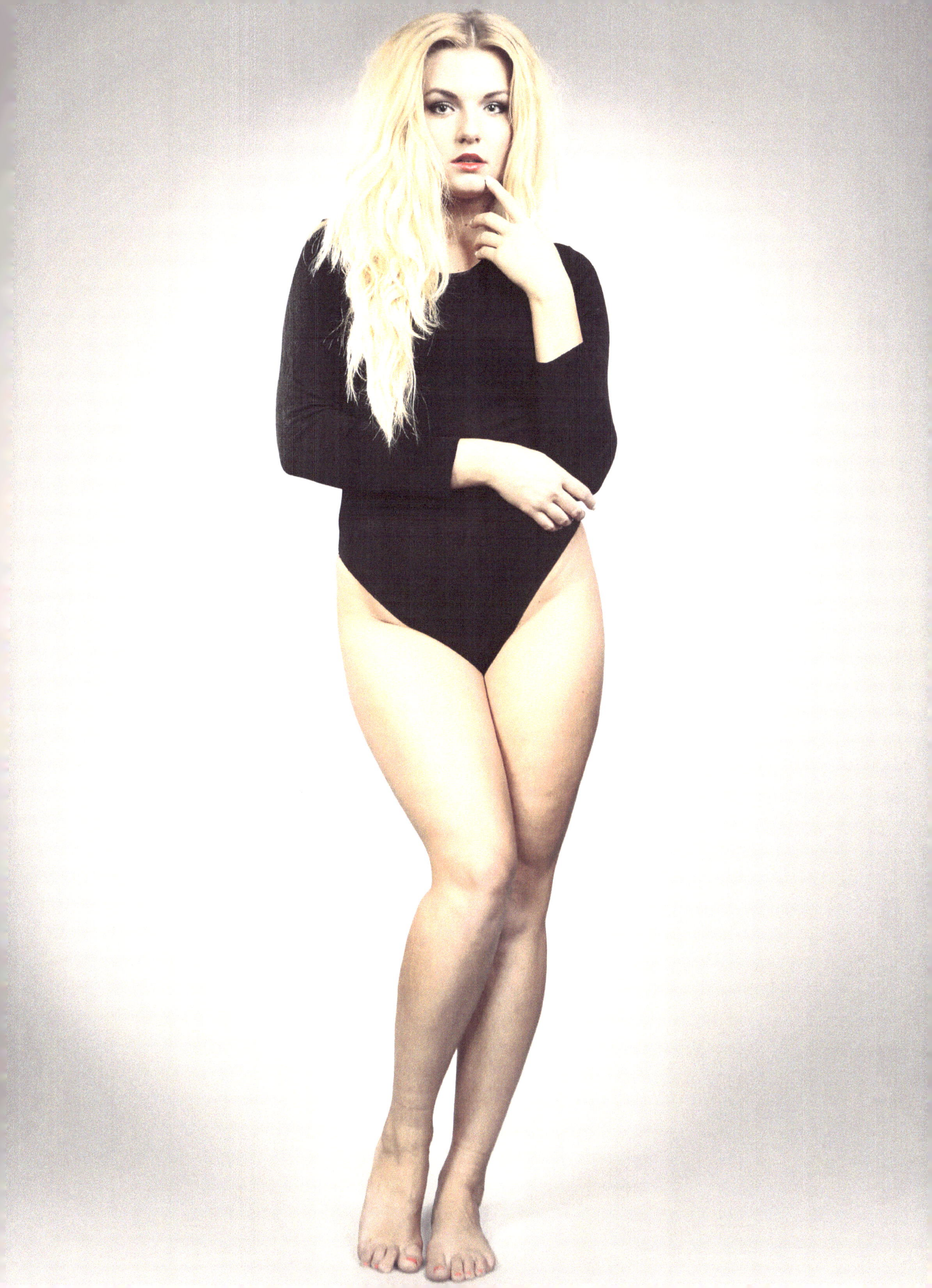

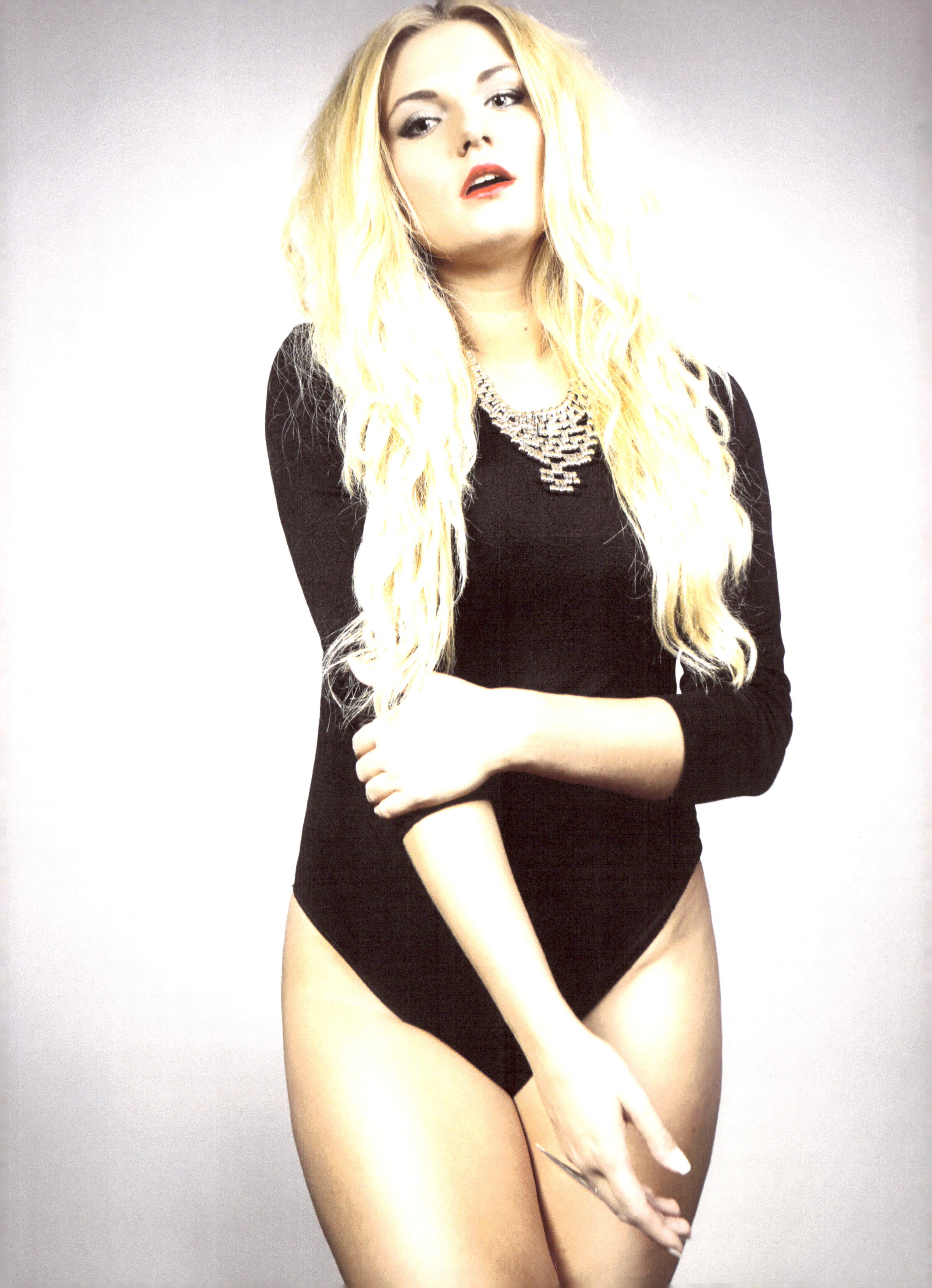

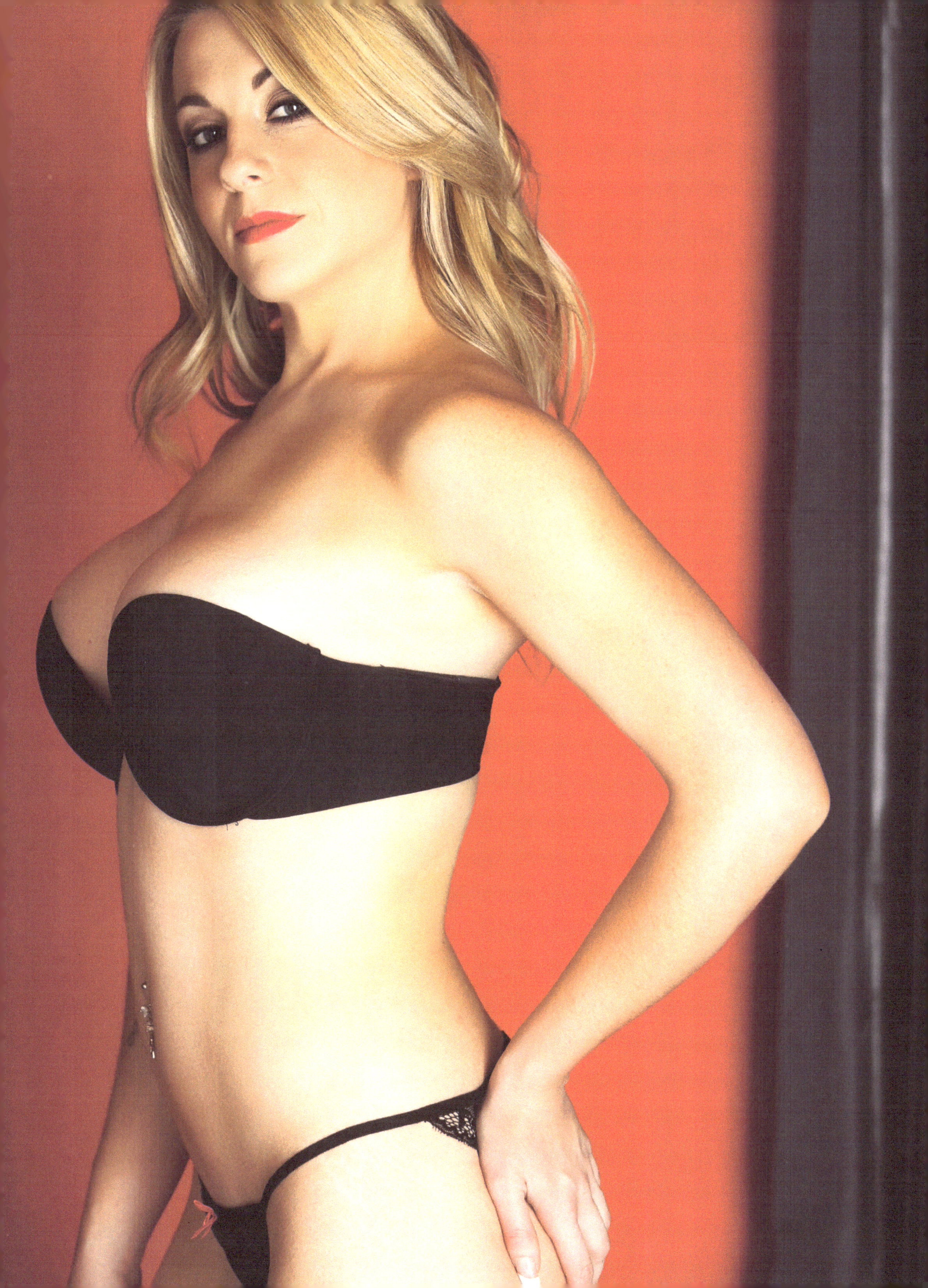

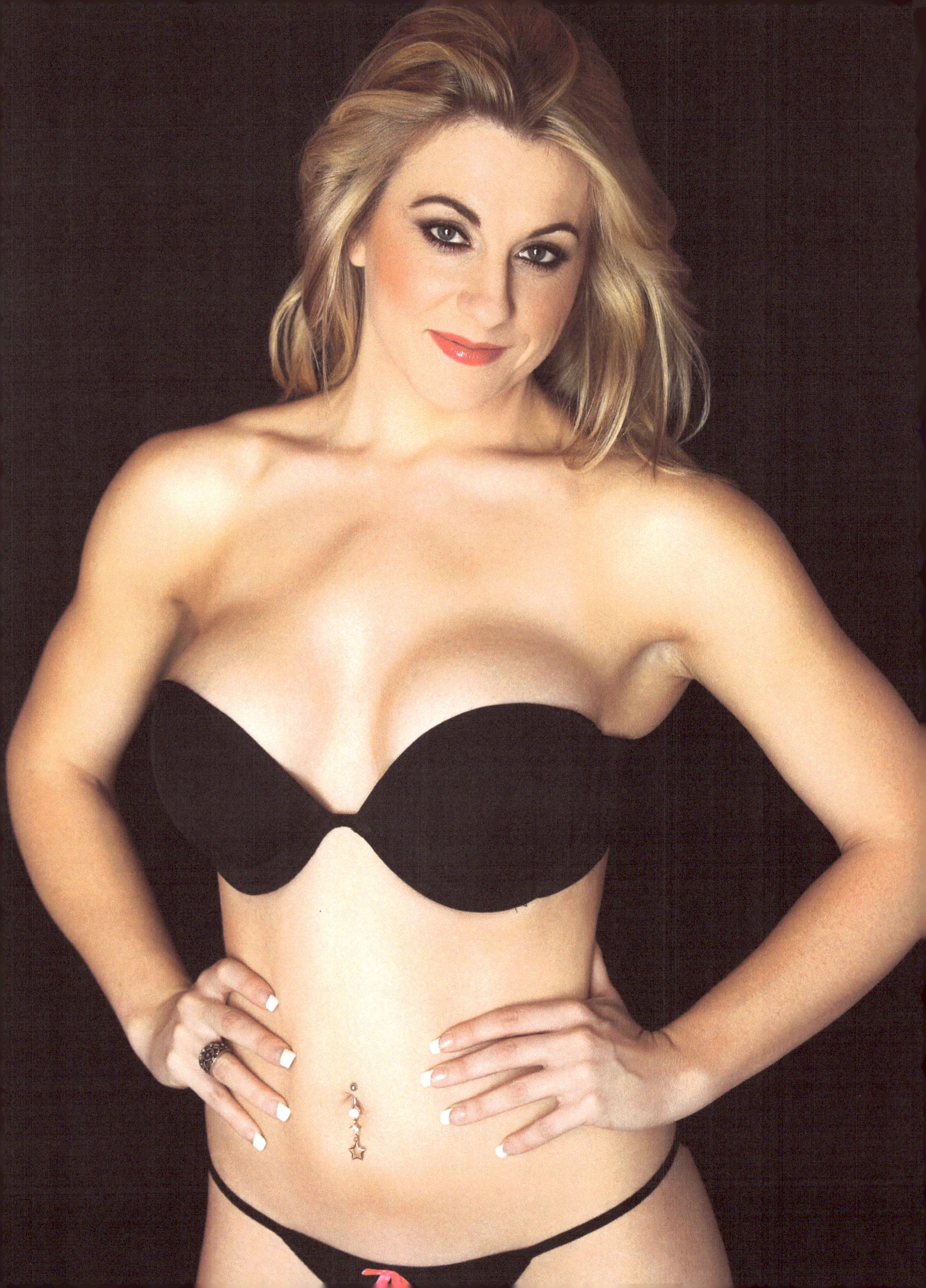

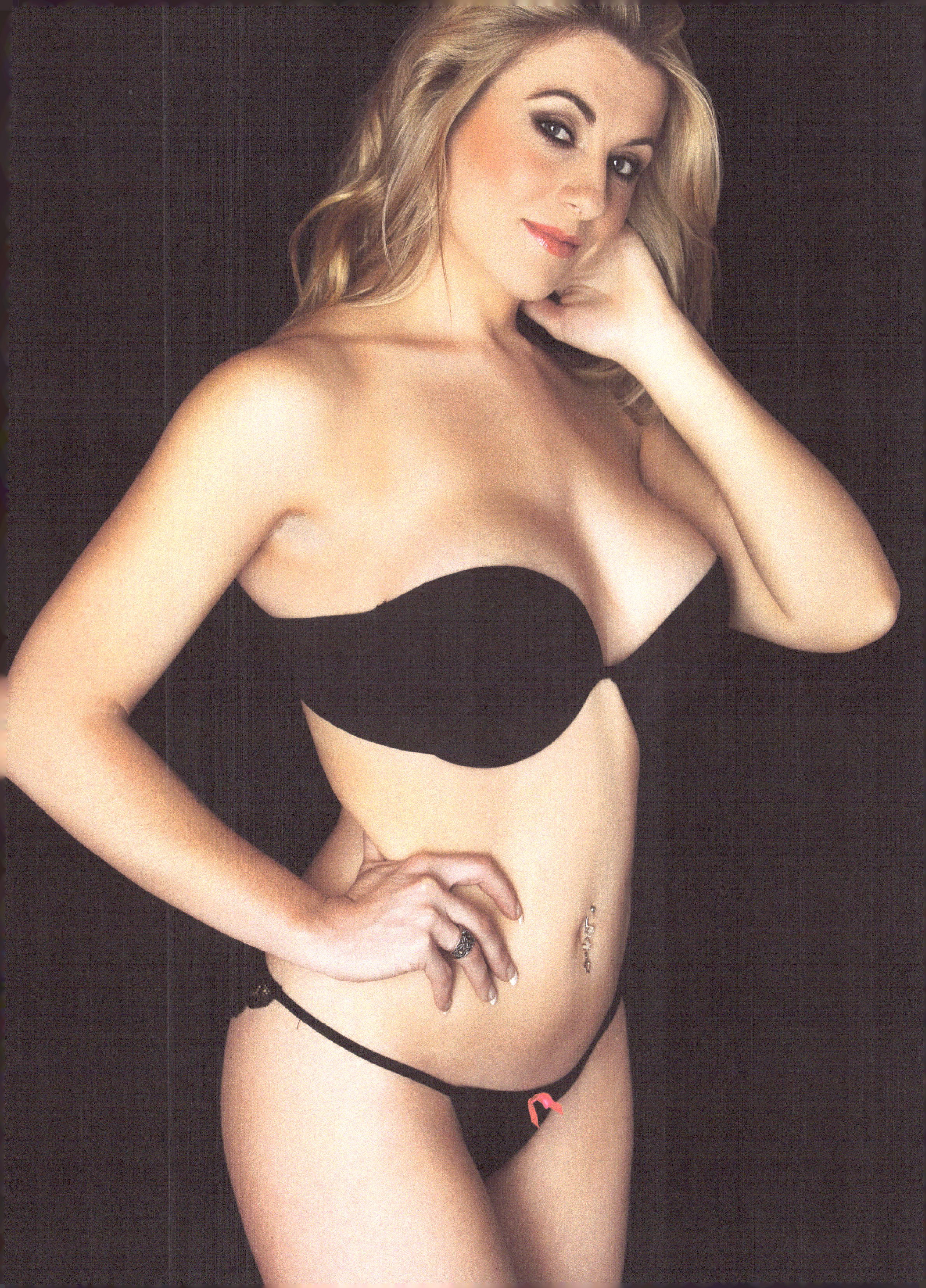

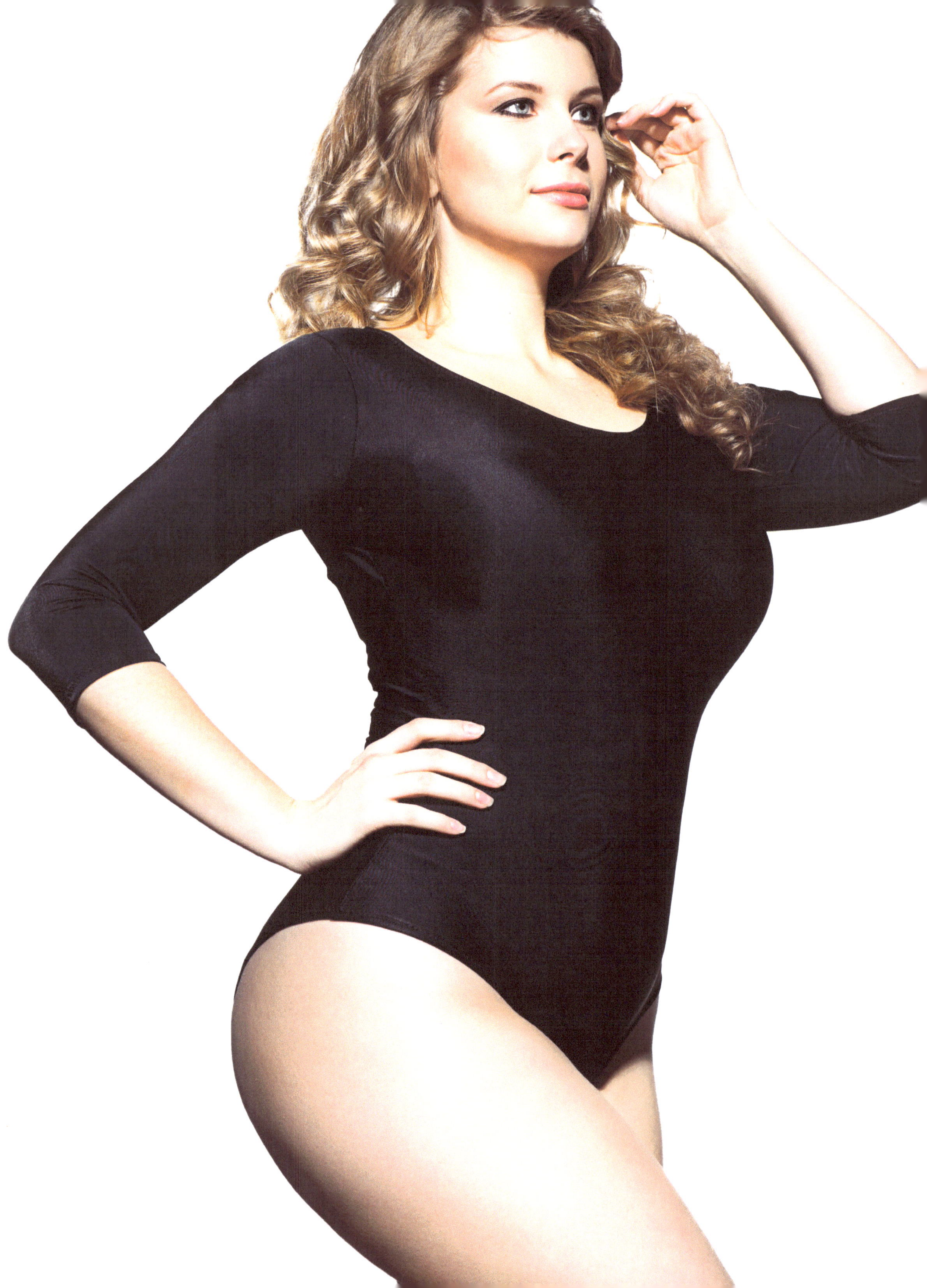

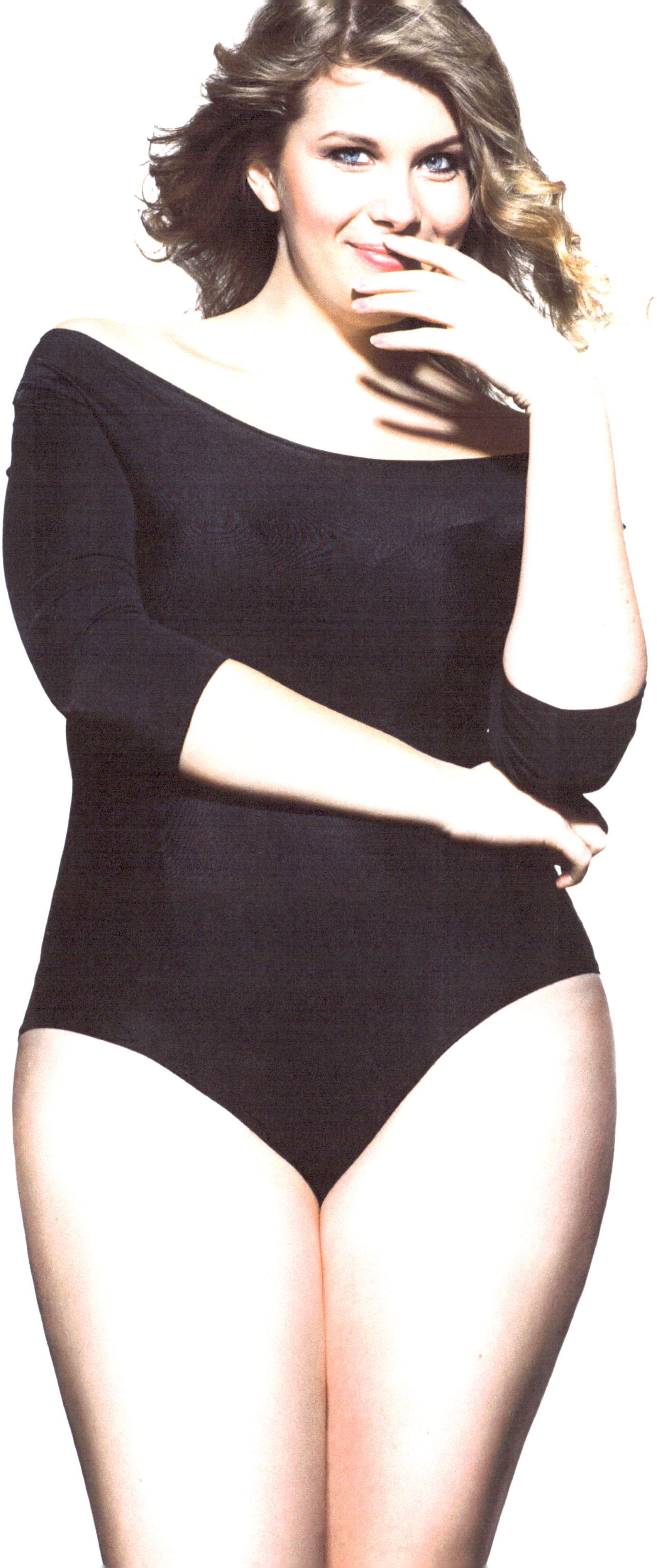

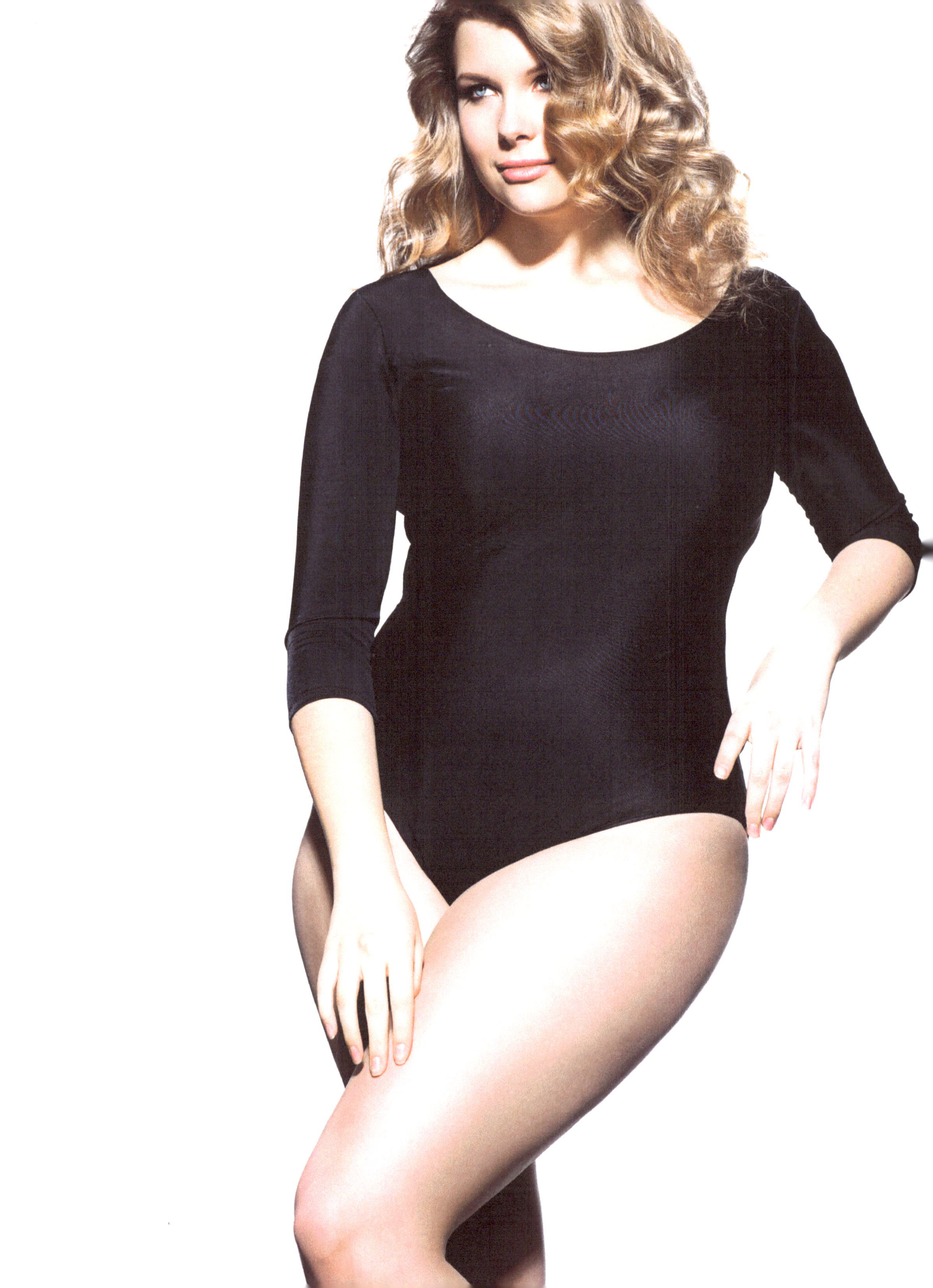

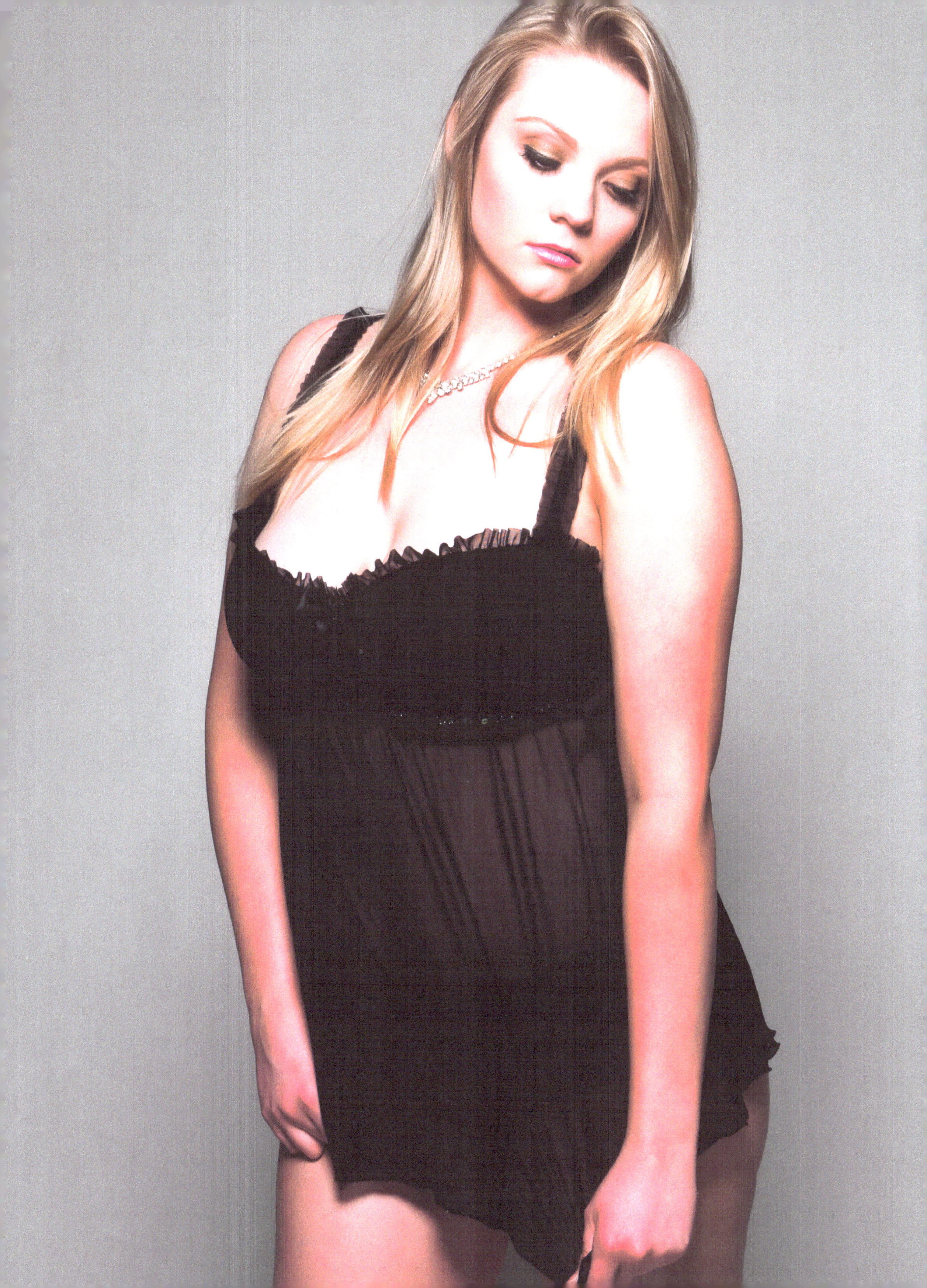

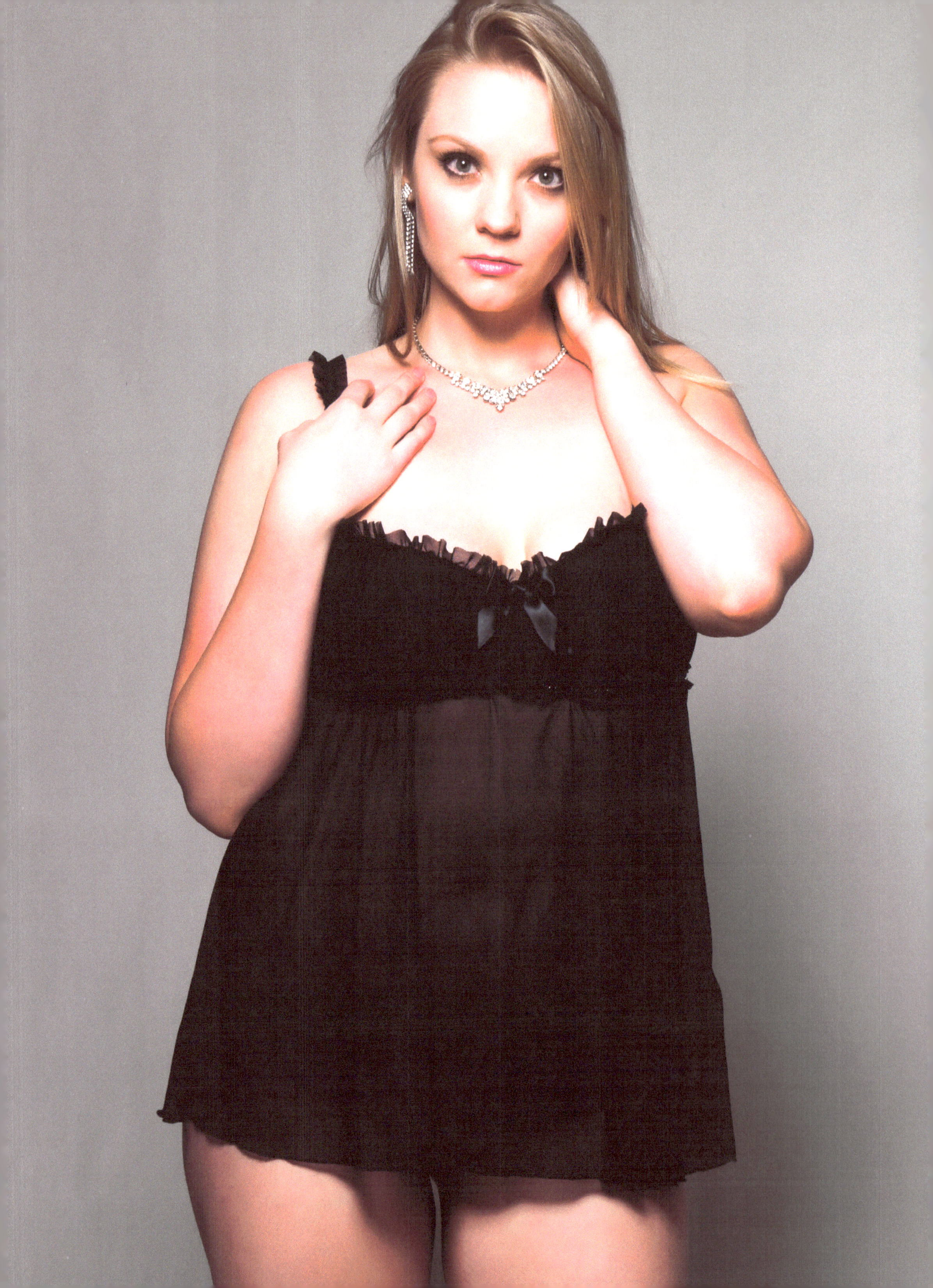

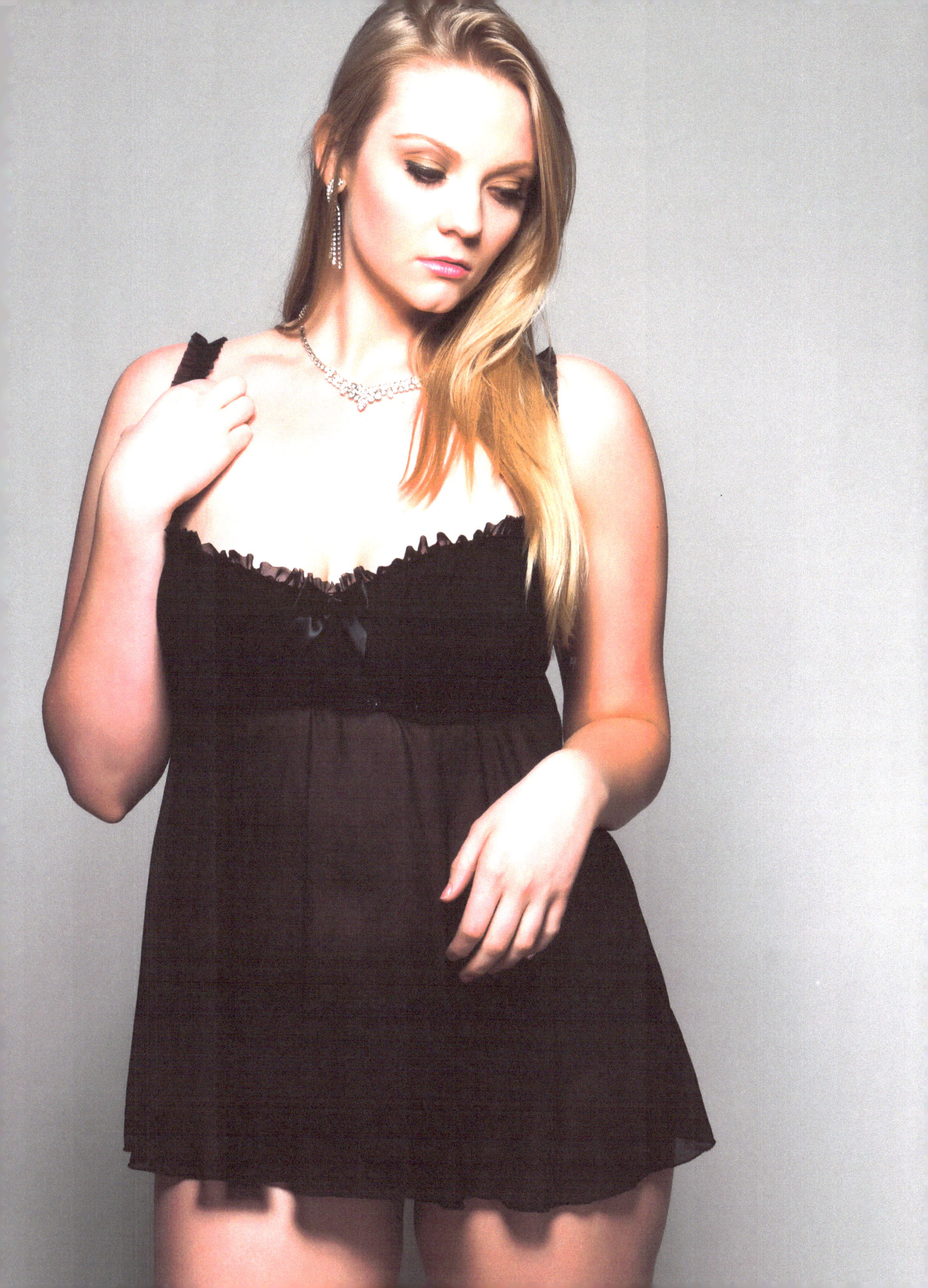

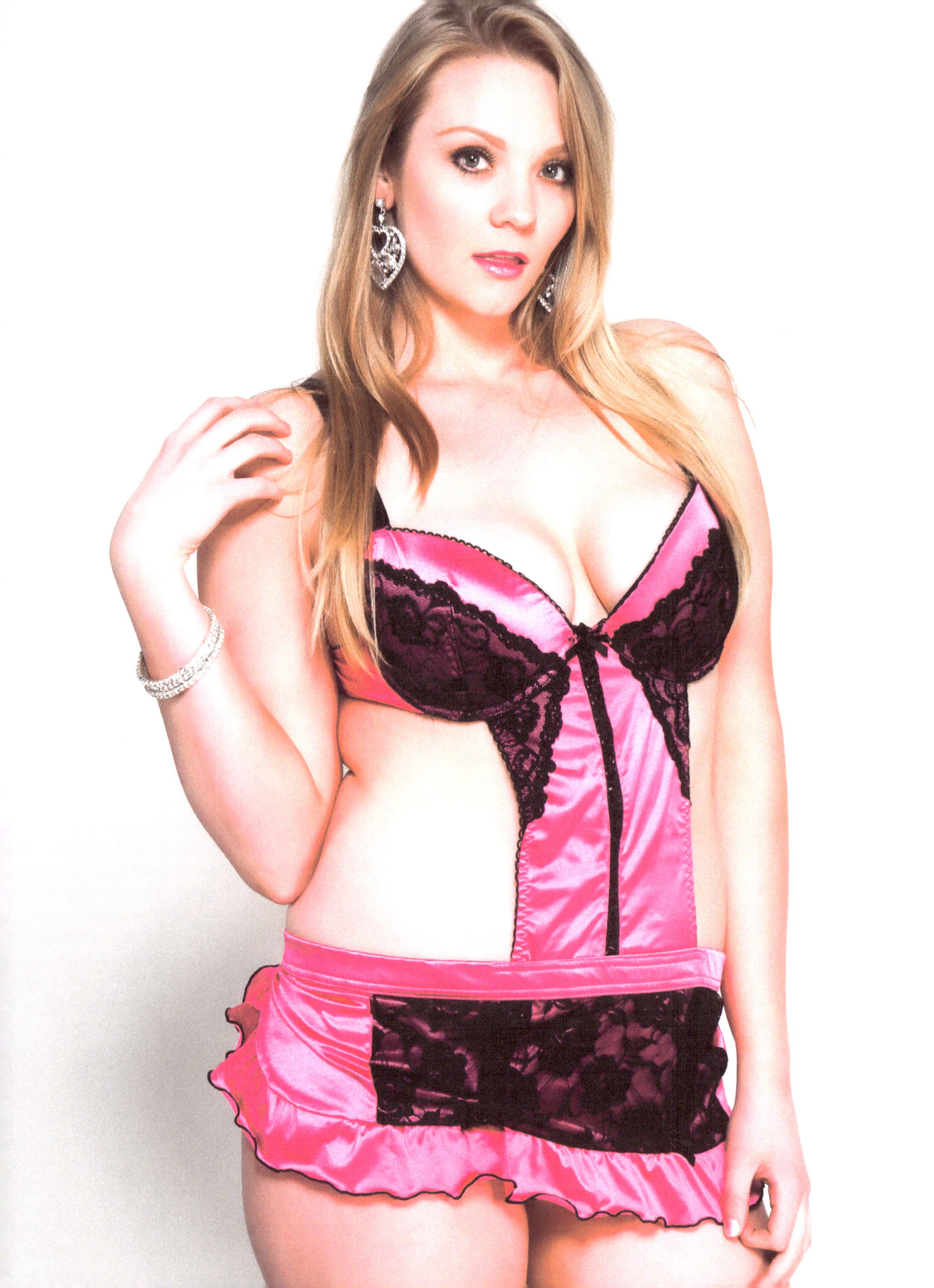

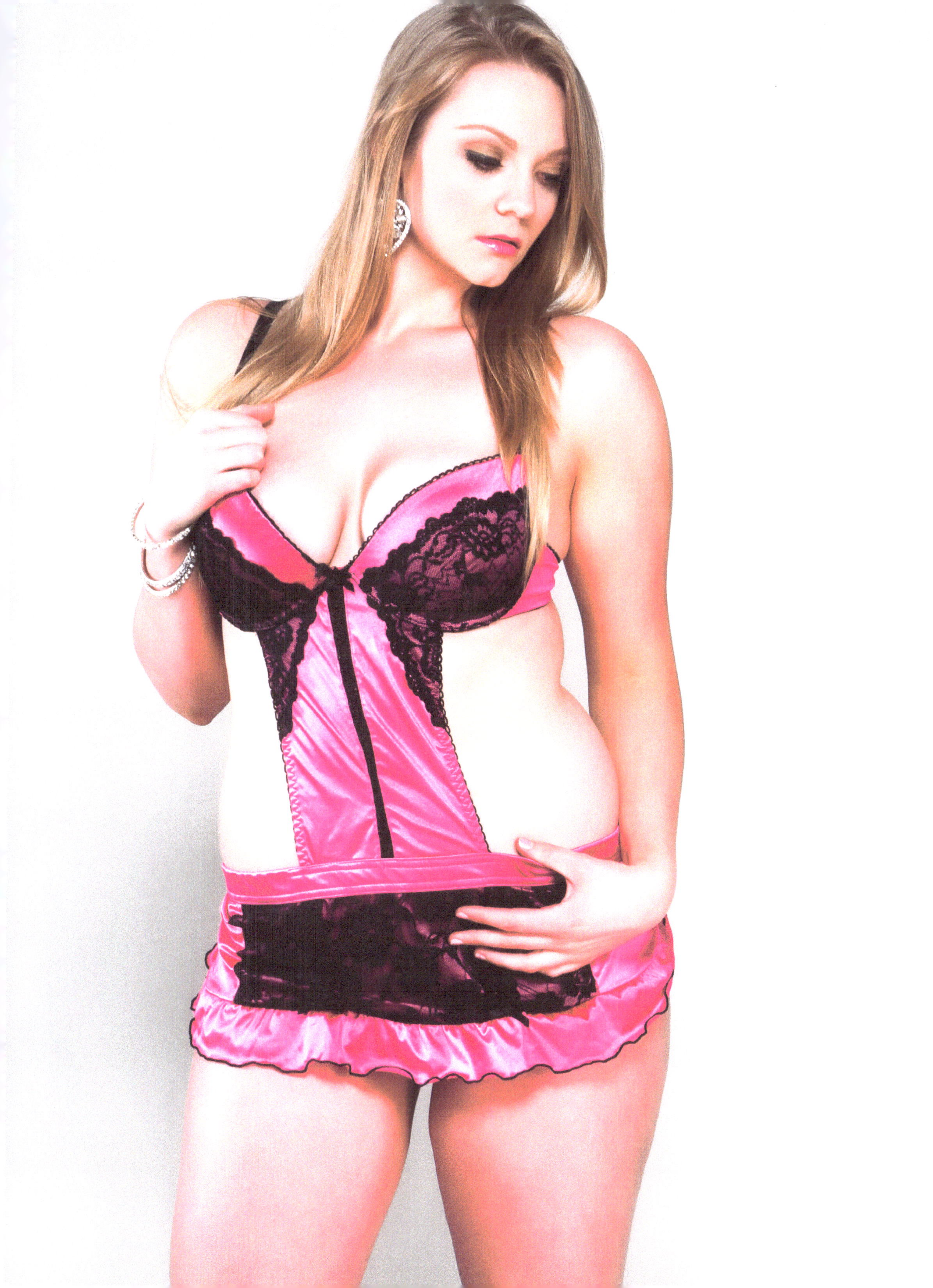

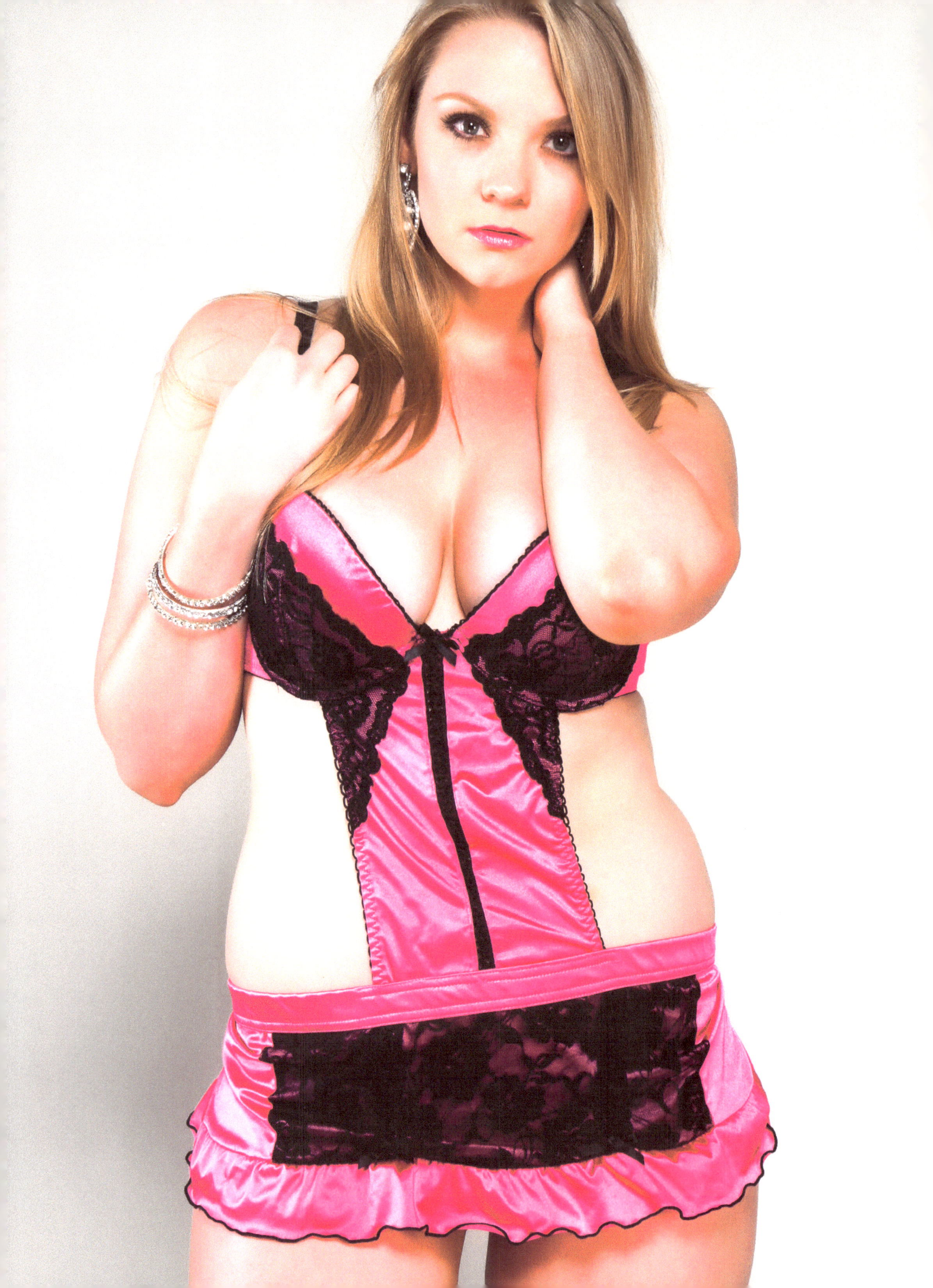

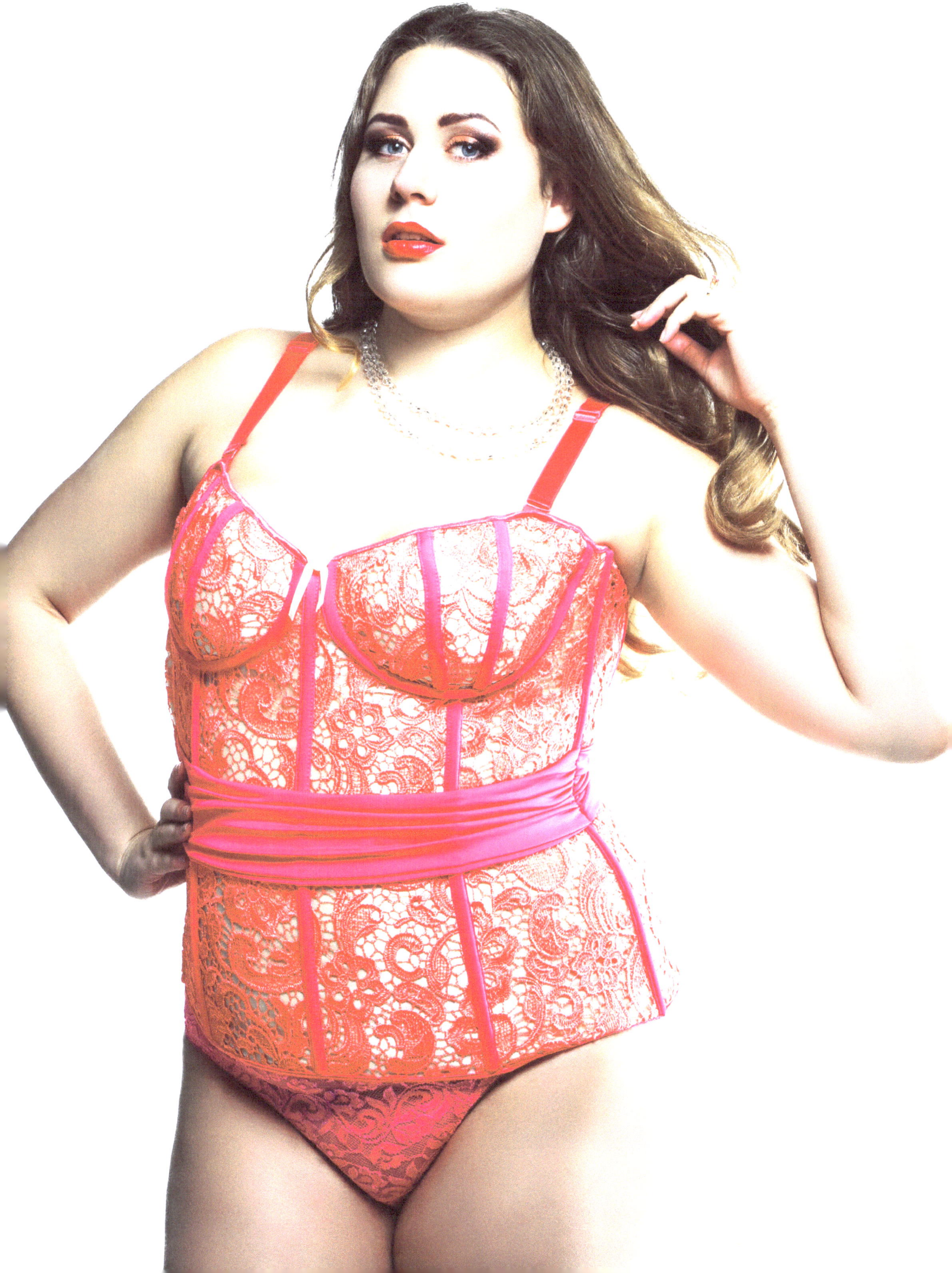

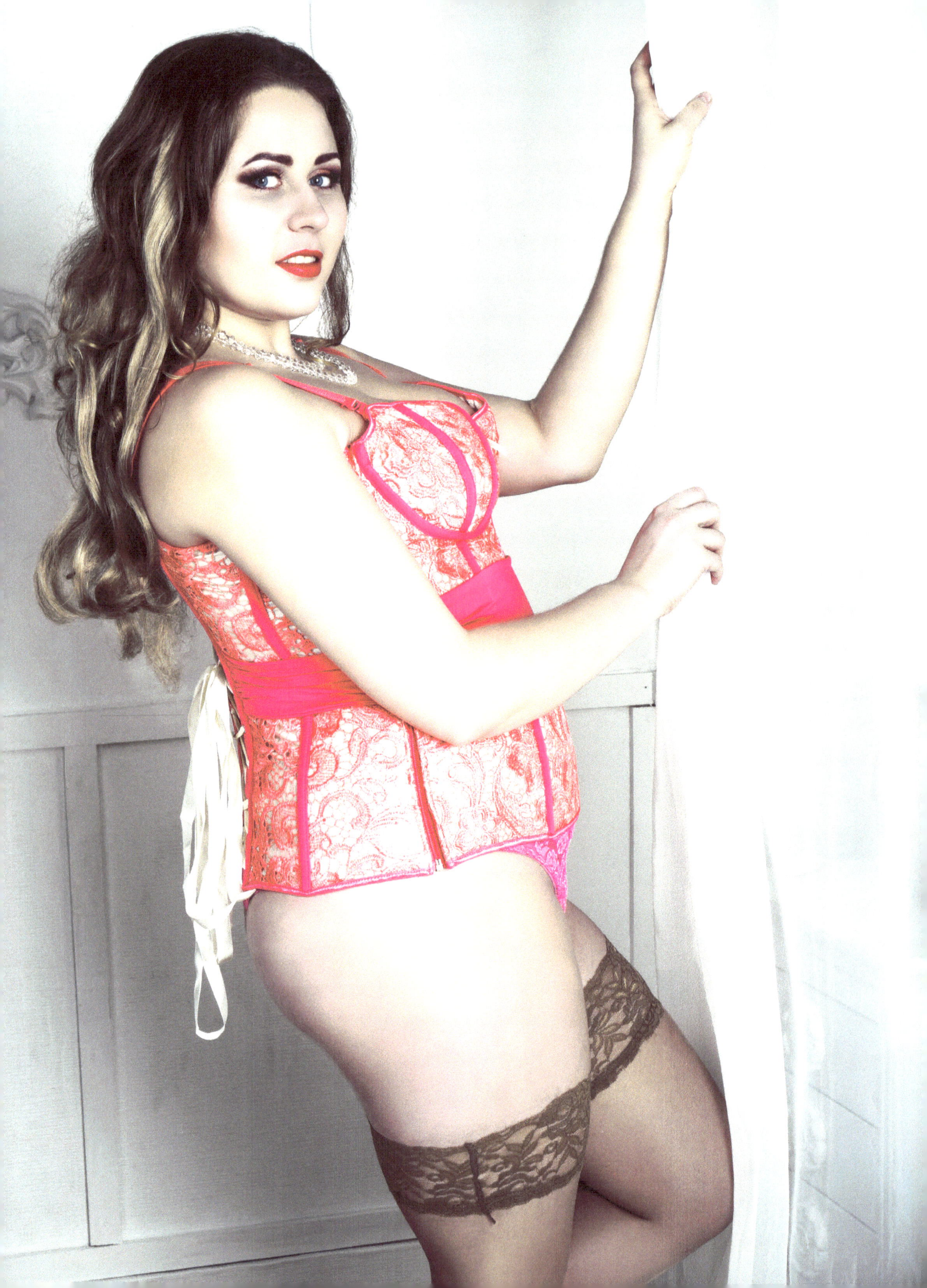

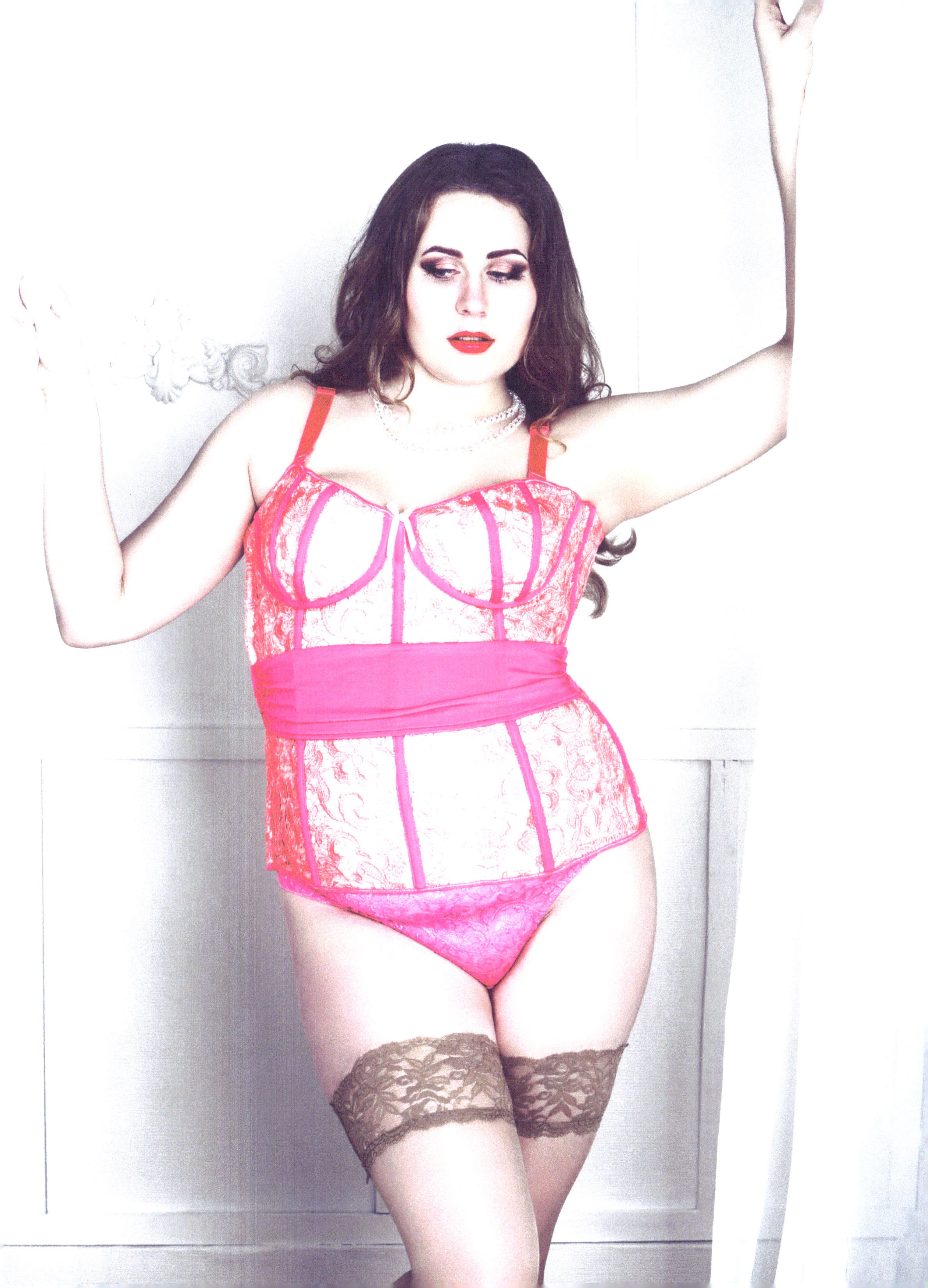

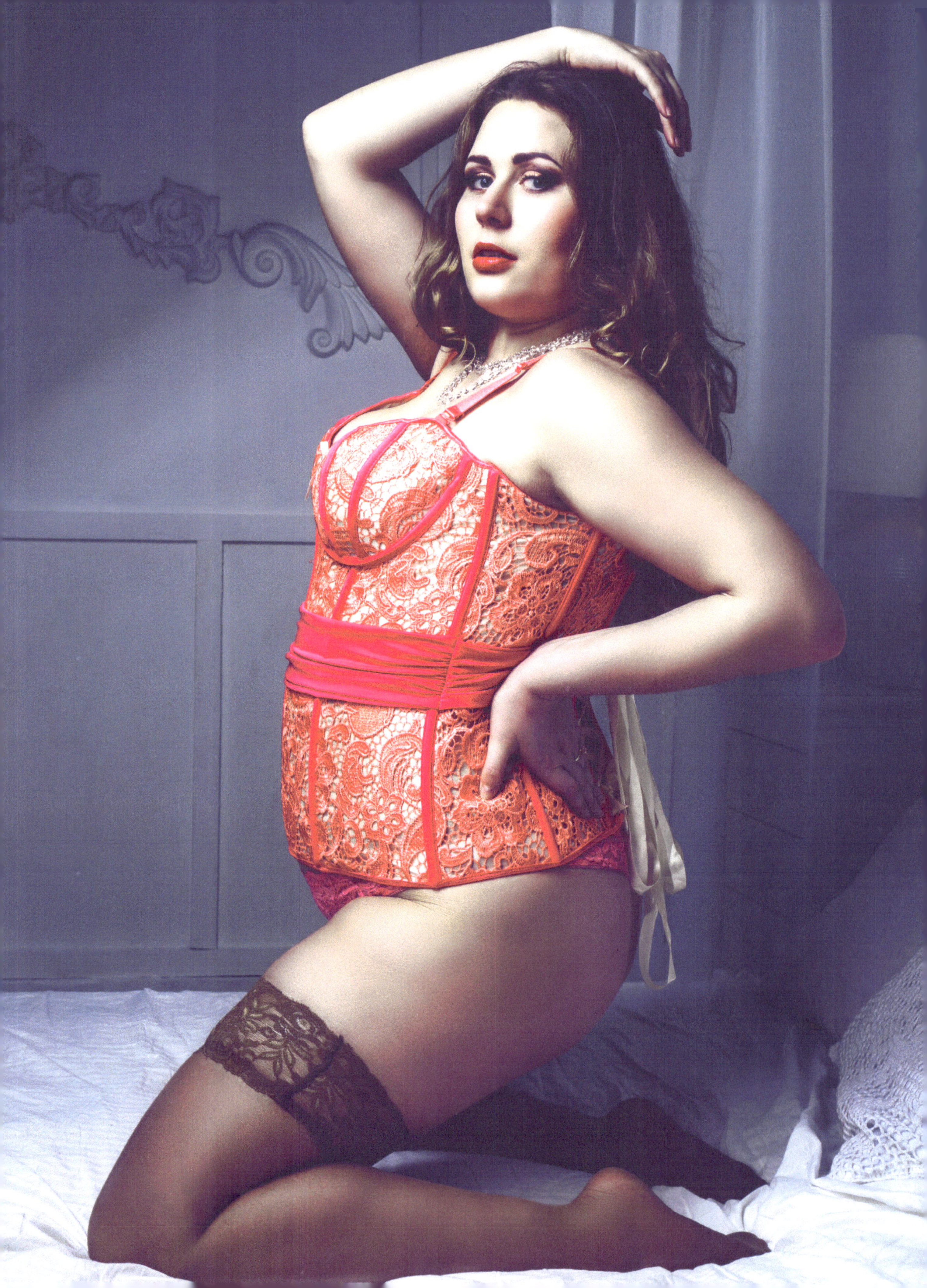

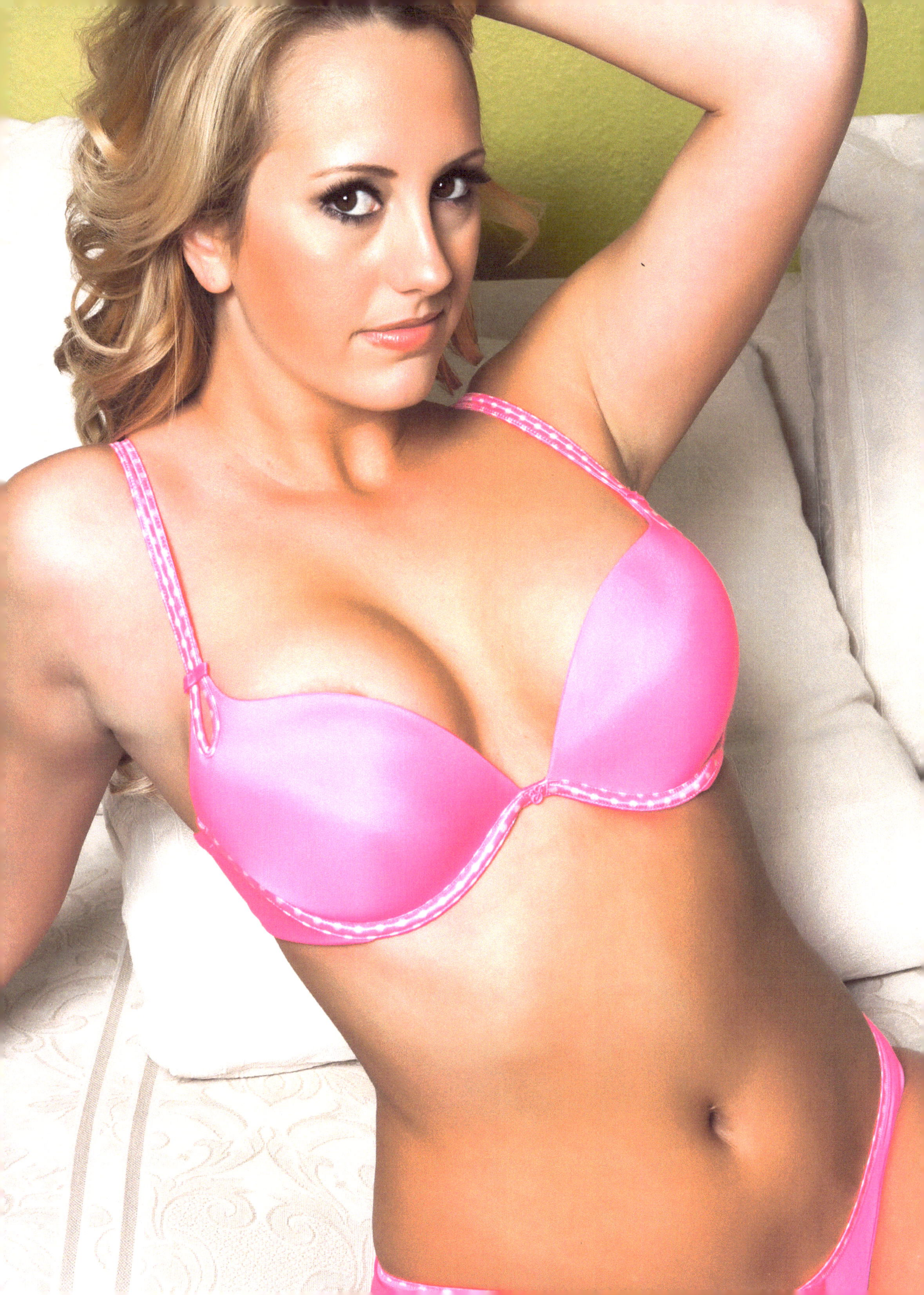

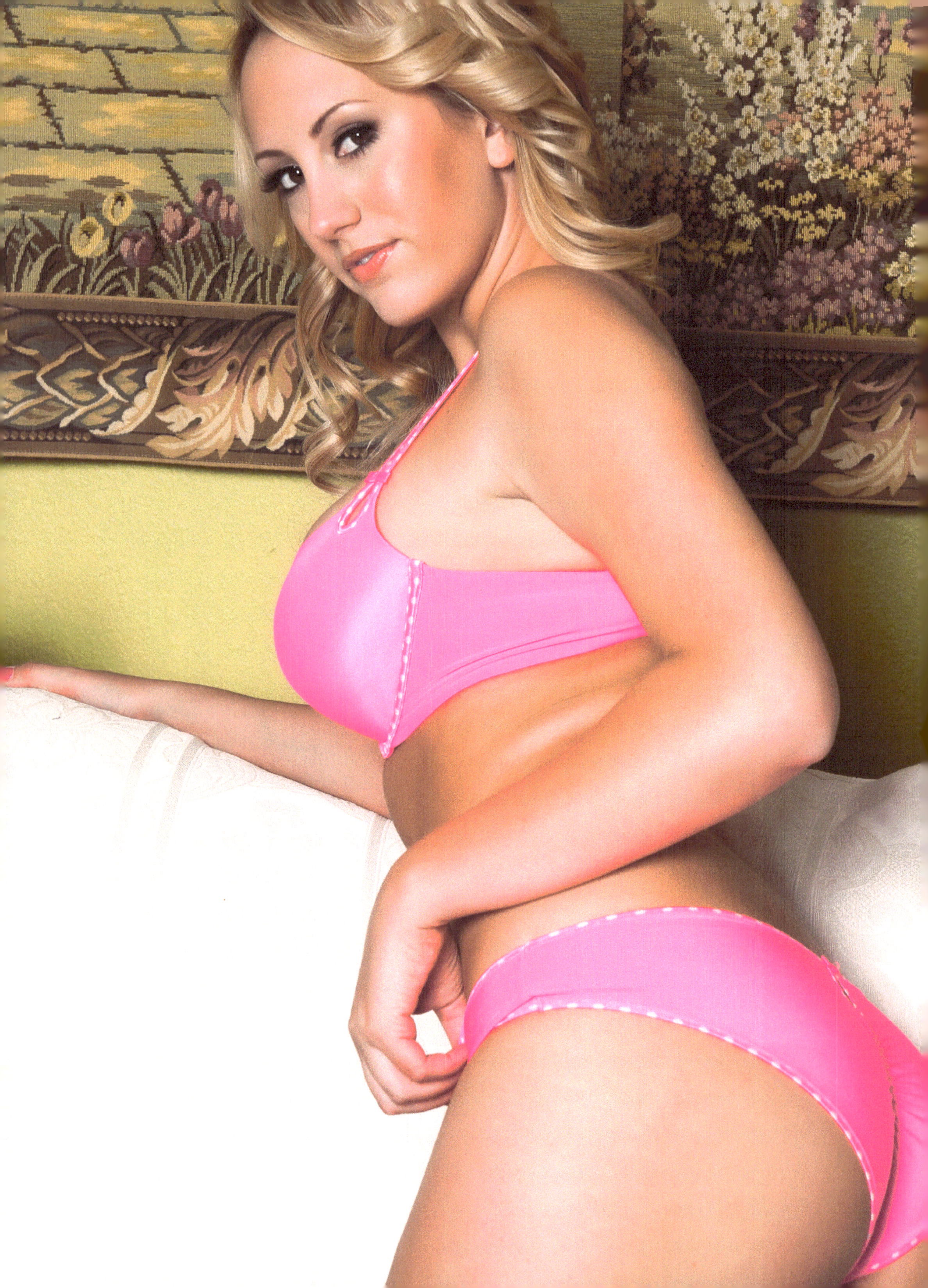

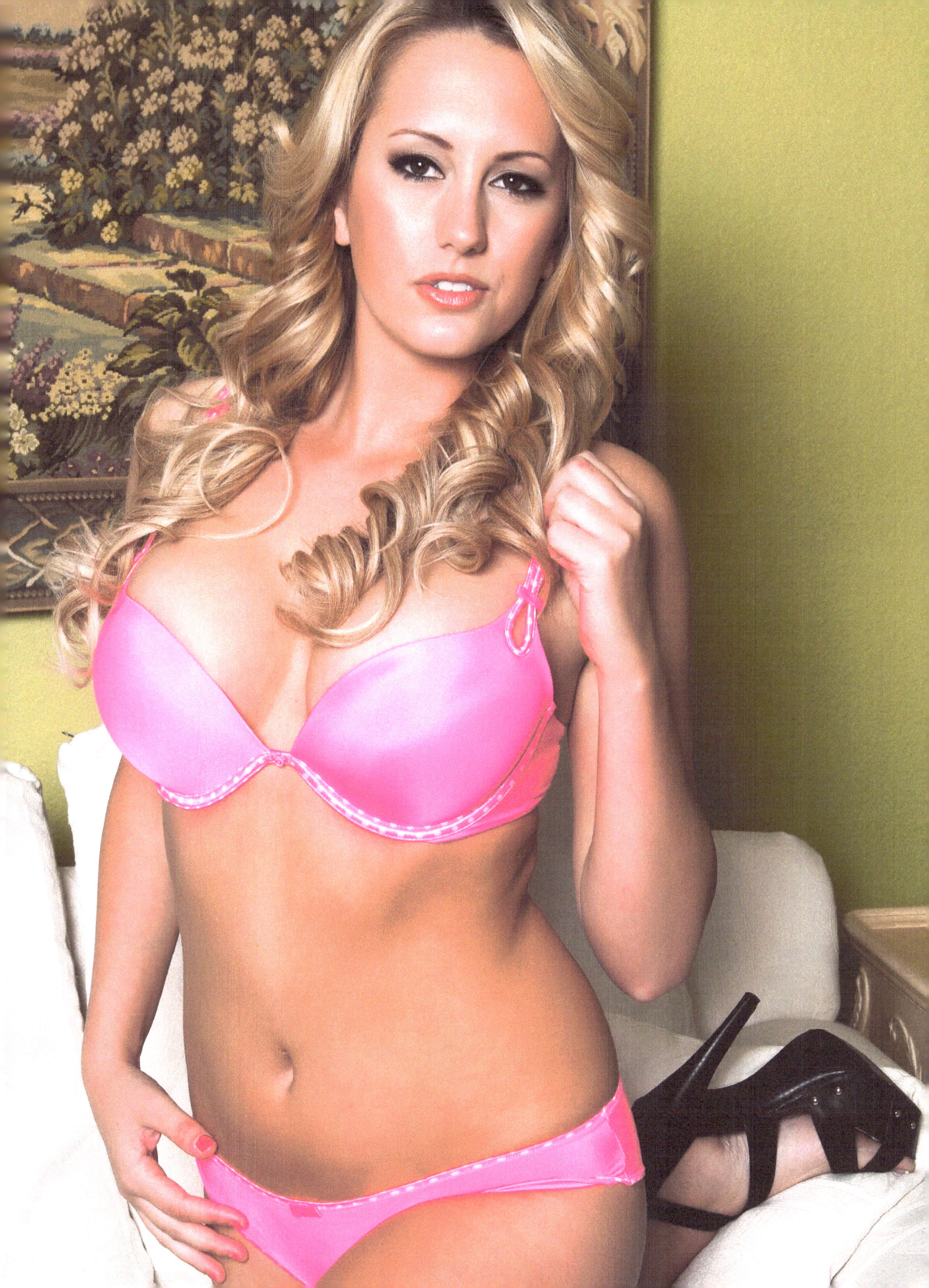

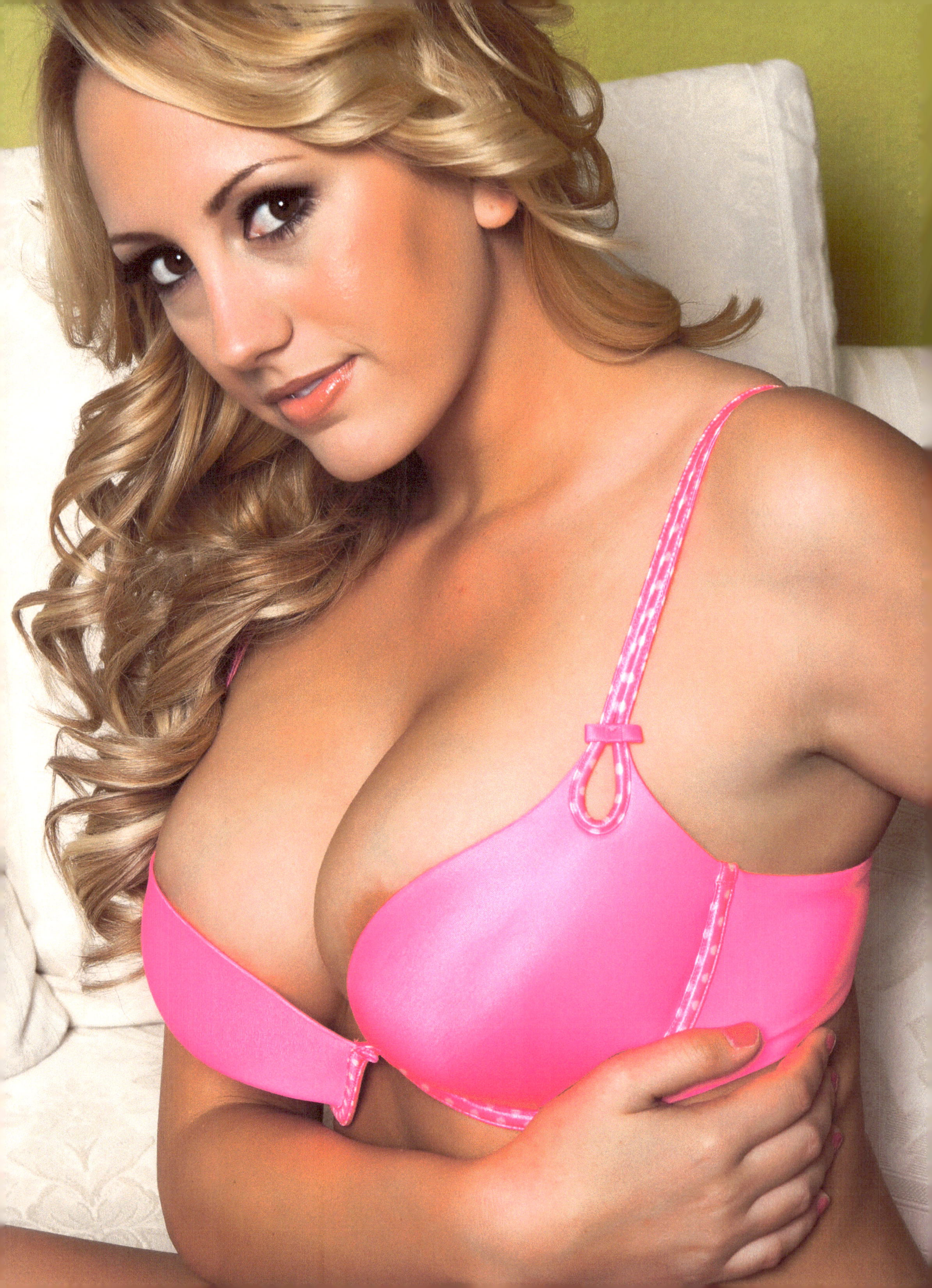

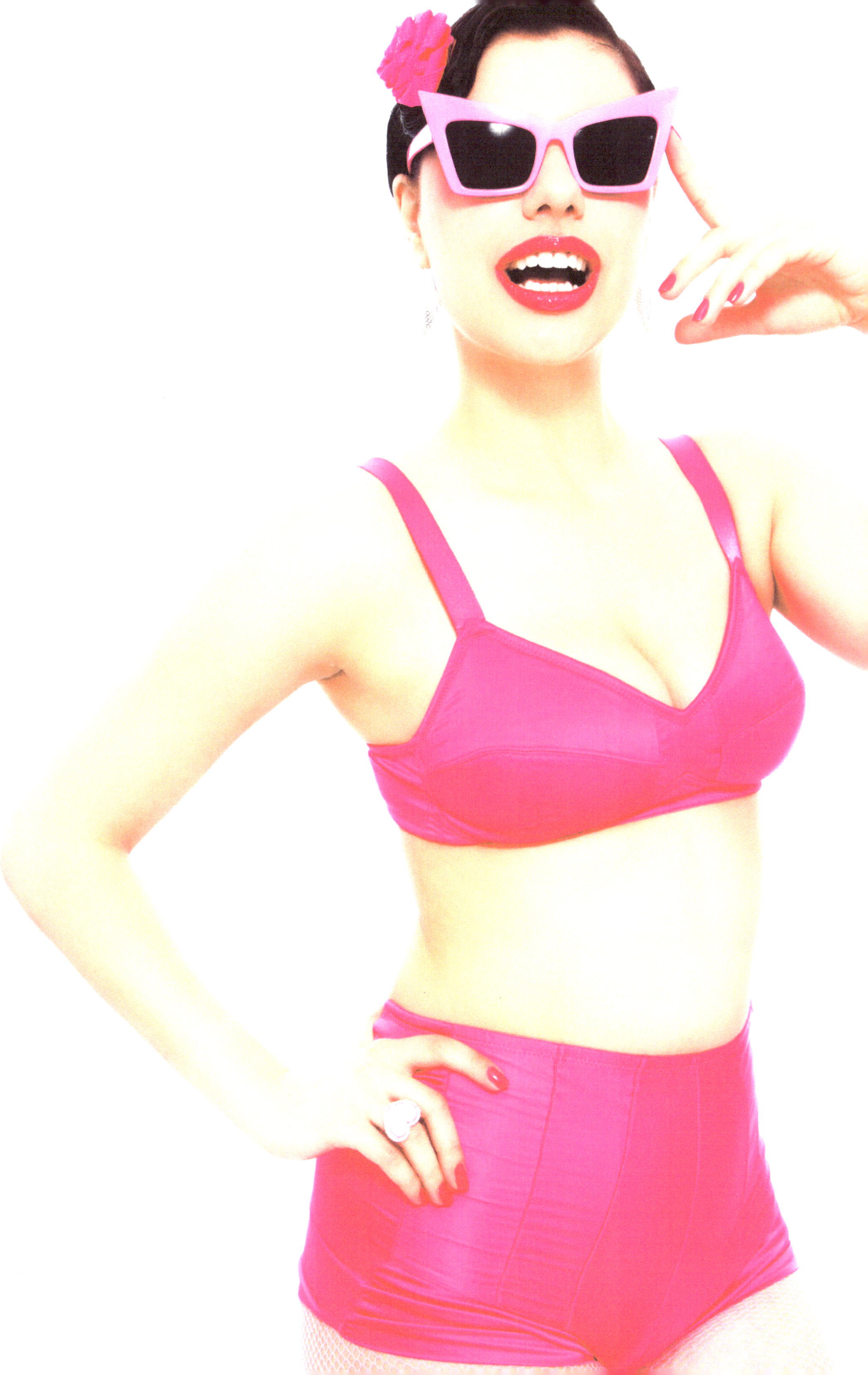

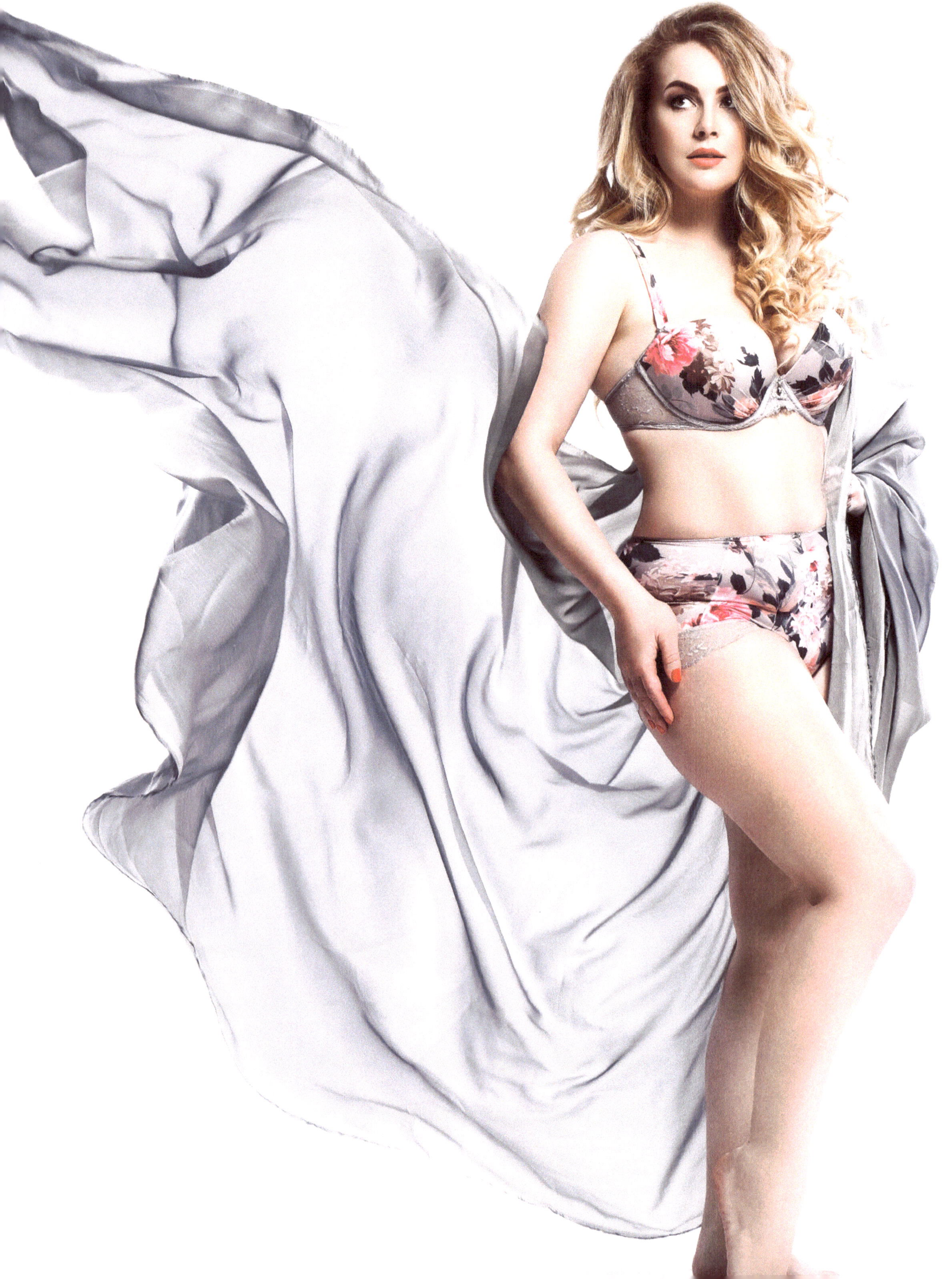

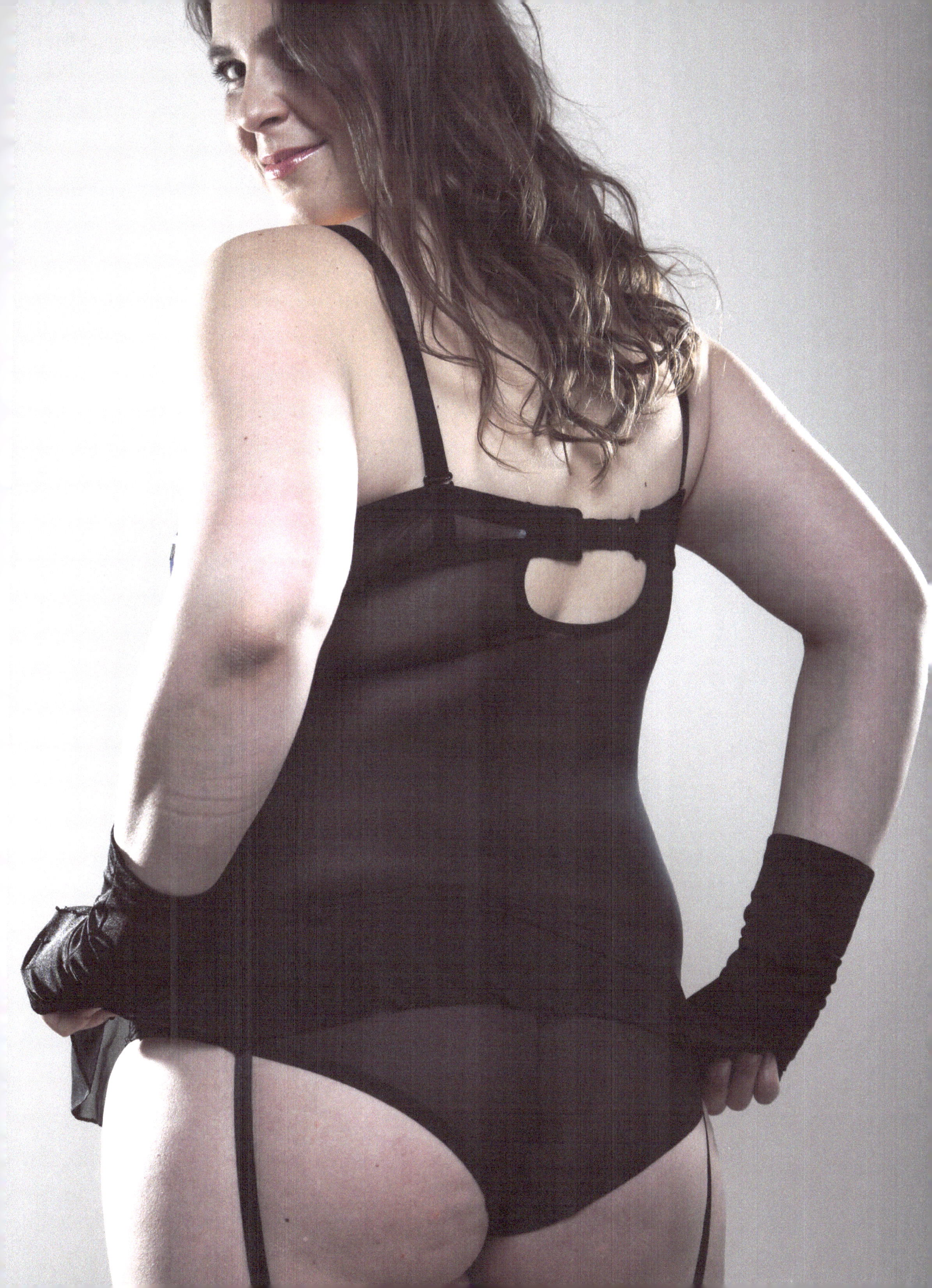

www.ingramcontent.com/pod-product-compliance
Lightning Source LLC
Chambersburg PA
CBHW050418180526
45159CB00005B/2323
* 9 7 8 1 5 3 9 6 2 7 1 7 3 *